Even though my lap is too small, my heart will always have enough Room for you...

Once upon a time in a cozy little cottage nestled in a vibrant garden, there lived a bright-eyed, brown-haired girl named Layla.

Layla was six years old and was known throughout her village for her boundless curiosity and her love for adventure.

One sunny morning, Layla found herself sitting in her grandmother's garden, making a sketch of the butterflies fluttering by while listening to the sweet songs of birds.

Her grandmother, tara, was a wise and gentle woman who had traveled the world and had many stories to share.

Layla's eyes widened with curiosity. "No, Grandma, what are they?"

tara smiled and patted the seat next to her.

"Well, my dear, the Five Pillars of Islam are like five magical keys that help us unlock the treasures of our faith. Let me tell you about them."

1. the First Pillar: Shahada (Faith)

tara explained, "the first pillar is Shahada. It's about believing in one God, Allah, and that Muhammad is His messenger.

It's like having a special key to our hearts that reminds us to believe in Allah's love and wisdom."

Layla nodded, feeling her heart glow with warmth.

2. the Second Pillar: Salah (Prayer)

tara continued, "the second pillar is Salah. It's when we talk to Allah through our prayers. It's like a magical connection to the heavens, where we can share our joys and worries with Allah."

Layla's eyes sparkled. "Can I pray, Grandma?"

tara chuckled. "Of course, my dear. You can start by saying 'Bismillah' and thanking Allah for this beautiful day."

Layla felt a sense of peace as she whispered her prayers to the sky.

3. the third Pillar: zakat (Charity)

"zakat is the third pillar," tara said. "It's like a key that helps us share our blessings with others. When you give to those in need, you spread happiness and kindness."

Layla nodded, her heart swelling with the desire to help others.

4. the Fourth Pillar: Sawm (Fasting during Ramadan)

tara told Layla about Sawm, the fourth pillar. "It's like a special treasure hunt for self-discipline, empathy, and gratitude. During Ramadan, we fast from sunrise to sunset, learning to appreciate the food and blessings Allah has given us."

Layla's tummy rumbled, but she smiled,
understanding the lesson.

5. the Fifth Pillar: Hajj (Pilgrimage to Mecca)

tara shared, "Hajj is the fifth pillar. It's like an amazing adventure to Mecca that Muslims undertake if they can. It's a chance to stand before Allah in unity, leaving behind our worries and sins."

Layla's eyes gleamed with wonder. "I want to go to Mecca, Grandma!"

tara nodded. "Someday, my dear. But for now, remember that every step you take with kindness and love is a journey towards Allah."

Layla embraced her grandmother, feeling the warmth of their love and faith.

As the days turned into weeks, Layla applied each of the Five Pillars in her life.

She shared her toys with her friends (zakat), prayed alongside her family (Salah), and even tried fasting for a day during Ramadan (Sawm).

One sunny afternoon, Layla noticed her elderly neighbor, Amira, struggling to carry groceries into her home. She rushed to help her without hesitation, and her act of kindness brought a smile to her face.

Layla's heart swelled with happiness as she realized that living the Five Pillars of Islam wasn't just about rituals; it was about making the world a better place, one small act of goodness at a time.

As Layla grew older, she continued her adventures, spreading love, kindness, and the wisdom of the Five Pillars to all she met. She learned that faith wasn't just a set of rules but a beautiful path to making the world a more loving and compassionate place, one adventure at a time.

Now kids, it's your turn to embark on an adventure of your own and dive deeper into the world of faith, friendship, and fun.

Are you ready to explore, learn, and have loads of fun?

Great! Let's get started. Choose any of the activity pages below, or try them all, and let your imagination soar!

Coloring fun

treasure hunt

Find and match the Five Pillars of Islam with their related image

 Shahada

 Hajj

 Salah

 Sawm

 zakat

Acts of kindness challenge

See below a checklist of good deeds you can start implementing. Let's see how many of these you acted upon this week.

☐ Greeting others with a smile (family, friends, teachers, strangers)

☐ Sharing toys with my friends

☐ Helping Mum and Dad with house chores

☐ Sharing something new that I learnt today with others

☐ Helping animals

☐ Being inclusive by including others in games and activities

☐ Keeping the environment clean (picking up trash in the neighborhood)

☐ Visiting elderly

☐ Donating (toys, clothes, items you do not use)

Design your own prayer mat

Let's get creative by designing our dream prayer mat...

Qibla

My Ramadan Calendar

Let's track the days of Ramadan by checking off the days of the month as they pass...

1	2	3	4	5	6	7
8	9	10	11	12	13	14
15	16	17	18	19	20	21
22	23	24	25	26	27	28
29	30	EID-UL-FITR				

Made in the USA
Monee, IL
27 May 2024

59015808R00024